# Holy Spirit My Best Friend

# Holy Spirit My Best Friend

## Wessel du Bruyn

Without limiting the rights under copyright(s) reserved below, no part of this publication may be reproduced, stored in or introduced into a retrieval system, or transmitted, in any form, or by any means (electronic, mechanical, photocopying, recording, or otherwise) without the prior permission of the publisher and the copyright owner.

The content of this book is provided "AS IS." The publisher and the author make no guarantees or warranties as to the accuracy, adequacy, or completeness of the content or results to be obtained from using the content of this book, including any information that can be accessed through hyperlinks or otherwise. The publisher and the author expressly disclaim any warranty, expressed or implied, including but not limited to implied warranties of merchantability or fitness for a particular purpose. This limitation of liability shall apply to any claim or cause whatsoever, whether such claim or cause arises in contract, tort, or otherwise. The reader assumes full responsibility for their choices and the results they bring.

Scripture quotations are taken from the following versions:

- **King James Version (KJV)**: Public domain.
- **New King James Version (NKJV)**: Scripture taken from the New King James Version®. Copyright © 1982 by Thomas Nelson. Used by permission. All rights reserved.
- **Amplified Bible, Classic Edition (AMPC)**: Scripture quotations taken from the Amplified® Bible, Classic Edition, Copyright © 1954, 1958, 1962, 1964, 1965, 1987 by The Lockman Foundation. Used by permission. www.Lockman.org

The scanning, uploading, and distributing of this book via the internet or any other means without the permission of the publisher and copyright owner is illegal and punishable by law. Please purchase only authorized copies, and do not participate in or encourage piracy of copyrighted materials. Your support of the author's rights is appreciated.

**Copyright © 2025 by Wessel du Bruyn. All rights reserved.**

Released December 2025

**ISBN**: 978-1-64457-811-7

**Rise UP Publications**
644 Shrewsbury Commons Ave, Ste 249
Shrewsbury, PA 17361, USA
www.riseUPpublications.com
Phone: 866-846-5123

# Contents

Introduction ... 9

Chapter 1 ... 13
*The Supernatural Church*

Chapter 2 ... 15
*A Calling from Birth*

Chapter 3 ... 19
*Encountering Jesus*

Chapter 4 ... 21
*Surrendering to the Call*

Chapter 5 ... 25
*Seven Years of Seeking*

Chapter 6 ... 29
*The Durban Encounter*

Chapter 7 ... 33
*Knowing the Holy Spirit Personally*

Chapter 8 ... 35
*The Dove and the Believer*

Chapter 9 ... 41
*The Mysteries of the Holy Spirit*

Chapter 10 ... 47
*Three Ways the Holy Spirit Comes*

Chapter 11 ... 55
*Suddenly, Everything Changes*

Chapter 12 ... 61
*He Is a Person, Not an It*

Chapter 13 ... 63
*Obedience and Intimacy*

Chapter 14 ... 67
*Natural vs. Spiritual Man*

Chapter 15    69
*Living with Power and Joy*

Chapter 16    77
*Holy Spirit, My Best Friend*

Afterword    87
Notes    91
About Wessel du Bruyn    92

# Introduction

This book is for the hungry—for those who are discontent and seeking what they don't yet understand. It's for the believer who knows there must be more to this life in Christ than simply attending church, following a religious program, and surviving week to week. It's for those tired of living beneath their spiritual inheritance—those who feel the weight of oppression, anxiety, defeat, or joylessness—and are ready to trade that in for the power, presence, and person of the Holy Spirit.

If you've ever felt like your walk with God lacks fire, wondered where the boldness, joy, and miracles of the early church have gone, and questioned why Christians often seem more defeated than victorious, this message is for you.

You were never meant to do this life alone.

## Introduction

The truth is, most believers know *about* the Holy Spirit, but they don't *know* Him. They've heard sermons, read Scriptures, maybe even experienced a moment or two of His power—but He remains distant, misunderstood, or altogether ignored in their daily lives. The encounters are brief, fleeting, and seem more accidental than intentional. This book exists to change that. You're about to be introduced to the One who was sent to live *inside* you, walk *with* you, pray *through* you, and fight *for* you. The Holy Spirit is not a force, not a concept, not a vague influence—He is a Person. And He wants to be your best friend.

Through these pages, you'll be stirred as I share my own journey. You'll be reminded of who you really are in Christ and who He really is in you. As I share my journey, you'll learn what it means to carry resurrection power, supernatural joy, unwavering boldness, and victory that doesn't fluctuate with your circumstances. You'll understand how to stop thinking like the natural man and begin living as a supernatural one.

If you let Him, the Holy Spirit will use this book to wake up your spirit, shake off everything the enemy has tried to bind you with, and ignite a fire in your bones that cannot be extinguished. You'll discover as I did that joy is not a mood—it's a weapon. That prayer is not a ritual—it's a power source. That your life is not random or small—you were born to carry the glory of God.

## INTRODUCTION

This book is an invitation. The Holy Spirit is already speaking. He's already reaching. All that's left is for you to say yes.

## Chapter 1

### The Supernatural Church

The greatest hour for the Church isn't behind us—it's here, right now. God is moving in this very moment. It's not something we missed in the 1950s or 1960s; it's unfolding today. In this final hour, what God is about to do on the Earth will be supernatural—beyond anything we've seen, heard, or even imagined. As Scripture says, *"No eye has seen, no ear has heard, and no mind has conceived the things God has prepared for those who love Him"* (1 Corinthians 2:9). I believe with all my heart that the Lord is raising up a supernatural Church, equipped and empowered for this time.

The early Church in the book of Acts was birthed in the fire of the Holy Spirit—and the last-day Church will be no different. Mark my words: the Church that rises before Jesus returns will walk in the same supernatural power, living in a continuous outpouring of the Holy Ghost. I believe one of the greatest restorations coming to the Body of Christ is the fear of the Lord—a deep, holy reverence that draws us closer to Him. The Spirit of God is returning in power to His people, just as He moved in the days of Acts. We are about to witness His glory and His miracles in ways the world has never seen before.

## Chapter 2

### A Calling from Birth

Before I was even born, doctors told my dad he would never have children. But my father—who is not only a preacher but also a prophet and a great man of God—held onto the promise of the Lord. He had always dreamed of having a son who would carry the gospel to the nations. And here I am—a living testimony of God's faithfulness. I grew up as a preacher's kid, a PK. And if you've ever wondered why PKs have a reputation for being naughty, I'll let you in on a secret: it's because we spend too much time playing with the congregants' kids!

My dad always dreamed of having a son God could use—and even though doctors once said he'd never have children, they were wrong. He and my mom had two daughters first, my older sisters, but his heart still longed for a boy. When my mom became pregnant with me, she didn't even realize it at first. She thought she had gallstones and went to the doctor. But instead of bad news, she got a surprise: "You're not sick—you're pregnant!"

My dad prayed earnestly, saying, "Lord, give me a son." He and my mom even asked God for a sign: if He was truly going to use me to preach the gospel around the world, I should be born weighing nine pounds—and with a frown on my face. Sure enough, I was born weighing exactly nine pounds... and yes, I came out frowning!

My mom later told me that as she was leaving the hospital with me in her arms, someone stopped her in the hallway and said, "God says He's going to use this boy all over the world." And just like that, the person disappeared. To this day, she believes it may have been an angel confirming the calling on my life. Growing up, I will never forget hearing my father's passionate, faith-filled prayers filling our house—they laid the foundation for everything I would one day become.

Children watch more than they listen—they mimic what they see. I grew up watching my father pray. I heard him cry out to God with passion and sincerity, and deep down, I wanted what he had. One day, while we were standing in a church, I heard people praying in tongues. I tugged on my dad's trousers and said, "I want that. Teach me that!"

He smiled and said gently, "Son, I can't teach you that. That comes from the Holy Spirit. But you can go into your room, ask Jesus to fill you with the Holy Spirit, and He will do it."

I couldn't wait to get home that day. As soon as we arrived, I ran straight to my room, closed the door, and dropped to my knees. With all my heart, I prayed and asked Jesus to baptize me with the Holy Spirit. And instantly, just as the Word promises, *"Out of his belly shall flow rivers of living water"* (John 7:38 KJV).

At the tender age of five, I was baptized in the Holy Spirit. I began speaking in tongues, and in that moment, I fell deeply in love with Jesus. From then on, something inside me changed. I developed an unquenchable hunger for God's Word. I read my Bible cover to cover, over and over again, and constantly asked my dad questions about Scripture. I devoured the Word, and even as a young boy, it became part of me—it lived in my heart. I didn't just know the Word of God; the Word was shaping who I was becoming.

## Chapter 3

### Encountering Jesus

I will never forget one night when I was just seven years old. I heard my dad crying out in the presence of the Lord. As I walked down the hallway past his room, I kept hearing his deep, broken prayers—and something inside of me pulled me toward that door. My dad never forced me to pray, but he showed me what a man of God does.

I stepped into the room, and it was pitch black—so dark I couldn't even see my hand in front of me. I felt my way toward my dad and knelt down, joining him in prayer. Suddenly, I heard a voice—a clear, unmistakable voice—say to me, "Look up."

When I looked up, I saw Jesus standing at the door. He radiated with the most beautiful golden light I had ever seen. I couldn't see His face, but I saw His body, and in that moment, I knew beyond a doubt: this is the One I will live for, the One I will give my life to.

An overwhelming peace flooded my soul—peace beyond anything I had ever known. At first, I thought maybe I was imagining it, so I looked away. But then I heard Him again: "Look up." I lifted my eyes a second time, and there He was—still standing at the door, brilliant and glorious.

That night changed me forever. He is beautiful beyond description. When Jesus walks into the room, everything changes.

## Chapter 4

### Surrendering to the Call

As I grew older, I began to rebel and drift away from God. I fell into a deep pit of depression—so deep that, at just twelve years old, I was planning to take my own life. The enemy wanted to destroy me before God's calling on my life could unfold.

I ran from the Lord and chased everything I wasn't supposed to. My dad always told me, "You're called to preach." But I pushed back every time. "I'm an introvert," I would say. "I'm shy. I will never preach."

At school, whenever we had to give oral speeches, I begged my mom to let me stay home. I told my dad, "I'll clean the church toilets, stack chairs, be a security guard, park the cars—anything—but I will never preach. Not ever."

I poured myself into sports instead. I became an excellent rugby player and even started boxing. I dreamed of playing rugby professionally. But at sixteen, everything changed. My body went into shock one day—I experienced stroke-like symptoms. My face pulled to one side, I couldn't speak, my hands stiffened—I thought I was dying.

My parents rushed me to the hospital, where doctors ran tests and discovered my stomach was full of ulcers that were about to burst. They said I needed immediate surgery to survive. But my dad refused. He prayed over me and declared, "Jesus will heal my son." The doctors ran another test—and the ulcers were completely gone. Jesus healed me instantly.

Yet even after that miracle, I still tried to outrun God's calling. I began drinking, getting into fights, and living recklessly. One day, during a fight, I broke my hand so severely that it required two surgeries with plates and screws to repair it.

As I lay in the hospital before the operation, I heard the Lord's voice clearly: "I gave you hands not to hurt people—but to heal them through the power of My Spirit." In that moment, I knew I couldn't run anymore.

Right there, I surrendered. "Lord," I said, "I'll do whatever You want me to do." I felt like the Apostle Paul when he said, "Woe to me if I do not preach the gospel" (1 Corinthians 9:16). My heart burned with a holy urgency. I knew I had to obey God's call—because if I didn't, I might not survive the weight of His purpose on my life.

That night, I prayed, "Lord, here I am. Send me." And He did.

## Chapter 5

### Seven Years of Seeking

I remember the moment I finally stopped running and said *yes* to my calling. My first time preaching was at a church of about 150 people. I came prepared—I had 18 A4 pages of notes spread out in front of me. I preached and preached with everything I had.

But nothing happened.

Some people even fell asleep during the service. I left discouraged and broken. When I got home, I went straight to my room, shut the door, and cried out to God:

"Lord, I told You I'm the wrong guy for this. You can use anyone else—why are You choosing me?"

And then God spoke something that changed my life forever.

"You have all the knowledge," He said, "but you lack the power."

In that moment, I surrendered again. I said, "Lord, I will not go unless You go with me. I don't want to preach without Your power. I don't want to be an ordinary man—I want the supernatural!"

I thought this power would just fall from the sky, but I quickly learned that it comes with a price. For the next seven years, I set myself apart. I prayed for hours upon hours every single day. I separated myself from people, from the world, and from distractions. I closed the door of my room, and I sought Him. Nothing else mattered to me—I had to know Him.

And I didn't pray until I was tired—I prayed until Heaven opened. I prayed until His presence filled the room. I prayed until I encountered Him. Many nights, my wife would come in and plead with me, "Please, come to bed. You're not sleeping anymore." But I would tell her, "I don't care about sleep. I want Him. I want the power. I must have the power."

I wanted to know Him—not just know *about* Him—but to know the power of His resurrection and even the fellowship of His sufferings. For seven years, I dedicated my life to seeking His face, and in that secret place, God transformed me.

The world desperately needs to know how to receive Jesus—but I also believe the Church must learn how to receive the Holy Spirit. Too many believers think of the Holy Spirit as an atmosphere, a feeling, or an idea. But He is a Person—our Helper, our Power, and our Friend.

The deep things of God require sacrifice. They require waiting. They require seeking. But when you step into that dimension of power, no demon in Hell can stop the assignment of God on your life.

You were not created just to exist—you were created to carry God's power for your generation. And when you carry His presence, atmospheres must shift. Wherever you go, darkness has to flee, chains must break, and lives will be transformed.

What a privilege it is—to be a vessel of His glory.

## Chapter 6

### The Durban Encounter

After seven years of intensely seeking the Lord, I was taking my team down to Durban, a city near the coast of South Africa. I was scheduled to preach, and on the way there, I heard God speak to me in a barely audible voice. He said, "From this day, I'm going to change your whole ministry. It will never be the same again." I asked, "Lord, what are You going to do?" But His voice went silent.

We arrived at the church, and I began leading worship. Suddenly, I heard Him say, "Open your eyes." When I did, I saw that every single person in the room was face down on the ground—no one was standing. Then He said to me, "You are next." I protested, "Lord, I can't be next—I'm the preacher. I need to preach the Word." But in that moment, I felt something hit me on the forehead. It was greater than electricity—an indescribable force of power beyond any natural explanation. I immediately fell to the ground—no one laid hands on me. I lay on my back, and my hands lifted into the air on their own. I had no control over my body. For two hours, I wept and prayed in tongues. I could not speak English. And during those two hours, God began to show me visions—people rising from wheelchairs, blind eyes opening, deaf ears healed, even the dead being raised to life.

While I was still under His power, the Lord reminded me of that moment when I was just seven years old, kneeling down and praying with my father, when Jesus stood at the door. And He said, "This will be the key to your ministry. When I become more real to the people than you are, healing will come. When I walk into the room, miracles will happen." I realized in that moment that everything I do must be fully dependent on Him. After two hours, they had to carry me out of that church. I couldn't walk, and I couldn't speak. I finally understood what the Apostle Peter meant when he said, "These men are not drunk as you suppose" (Acts 2:15). I was drunk—but not with wine. I was filled with the power of the Holy Spirit.

From that day forward, everything changed. After seven years of weeping, seeking, and longing, the miracles began. But the key ingredient wasn't the method—it was the power that flows from a true encounter with the Holy Spirit. I have witnessed with my own eyes how this power raises the dead.

One day, I received a call from a family whose loved one had passed away in the hospital. My wife and I went to the hospital room, where the family stood around the body in grief. A nurse showed us his lifeless body and told us he had died some time ago—there was nothing more that could be done. She even took a flashlight and shone it directly into his eyes to show there was no response. I looked at her and asked, "Can we just have two minutes?" I turned to my wife and said, "Let's pray." I laid my hands on him and said, "Father, in the name of Jesus…" and instantly we felt a surge of power ripple through that hospital room. It was as if the entire building trembled. Suddenly, the man sat bolt upright, screaming, yanking the tubes from his throat. We serve a wonderful Jesus who has given us power over death!

Let me say this plainly: that kind of power doesn't come through eloquence or titles. Power comes from encounter. True power is the result of communion with the Holy Spirit—what the Bible calls *dunamis*[i] power. But many people seek the Holy Spirit only for His power, without realizing He desires relationship above all. He's not an atmosphere or a mere force—He's a Person, and He wants to walk with us, speak to us, and move through us.

I want Him. I want the Holy Spirit. I want that anointing. I want that power. God the Father is in charge of operation, Jesus is in charge of administration, and the Holy Spirit is in charge of manifestation.

I like to imagine that in the dateless past, when God planned humanity, there was a boardroom meeting in Heaven. God the Father said, "Let Us make man in Our image and likeness, and let Us give him dominion over the earth" (Genesis 1:26). But God knew man would fail, and that the blood of bulls and goats would never be enough to redeem him; man needed a savior. So God the Word—Jesus—stepped forward and said, "Send Me. I will become the ultimate sacrifice."

But then He turned to God the Spirit—the Holy Spirit—and said, "I'm going to need You to take Me and turn Me into seed, and place Me inside the womb of a virgin. I'm going to need You to anoint Me, and when the time comes, I'll need You to raise Me from the dead" (See Acts 10:38).

Now think about this: If the Holy Spirit is powerful enough to take God and turn Him into seed—imagine what He can do with you! The Holy Spirit took the Son of God and made Him the Son of Man. And today, He's still taking sons of men and transforming them into sons of God.

## Chapter 7

### Knowing the Holy Spirit Personally

If you're waiting for goosebumps, you're in the wrong place—because the Holy Spirit isn't in the goosebumps business. He's in the *changing* business. He doesn't come just to make us feel good; He comes to transform us. The Holy Spirit changes us from the inside out. He turns monuments into movements. He takes what is stagnant and breathes life into it.

The Holy Spirit is not a force or an energy—He is a person, more real than the person sitting next to you. And as a person, He has emotions. He can be grieved. He desires a relationship. He speaks, leads, and reveals the heart of the Father.

One of the most powerful revelations I've come to after years of pursuing His presence is this: The Holy Spirit has feelings. He's not some vague presence floating in the atmosphere—He's the ever-present friend of Jesus and the indwelling power of God in our lives.

When Jesus came to the Earth, the Bible says:

> How God anointed Jesus of Nazareth
> with the Holy Spirit and with power,
> who went about doing good and
> healing all who were oppressed by the
> devil, for God was with Him.
>
> — ACTS 10:38 (NKJV)

Think about that. Jesus—fully God, yet fully human—needed the Holy Spirit while He walked on this Earth. If He needed to be anointed by the Holy Spirit to fulfill His mission, how much more should we cry out to be anointed by Him?

We cannot fulfill our calling without Him. We cannot live a victorious life without Him. We cannot walk in power without Him. The Holy Spirit is not optional—He is essential. And He's not distant. He's waiting for a relationship.

## Chapter 8

### The Dove and the Believer

Scripture tells us in the Gospels that when Jesus was baptized, the Holy Spirit descended from Heaven in the form of a dove and rested upon Him. But it is the Gospel of John that gives us a deeper understanding—it says the Spirit came and *remained* on Him. That's a key distinction. The Spirit didn't just visit Jesus; He stayed.

Many Christians understand that when you give your life to Jesus, the Holy Spirit comes to dwell within you. This is the seal of salvation—the promise that you belong to Him. But far fewer understand that Jesus came not only to save us, but to baptize us with the Holy Spirit and fire.

The truth is, most believers have the Spirit, but they lack the fire. They're sealed for Heaven, but they're not burning with power. When you're truly introduced to the Holy Spirit, zeal begins to consume you.

> Because zeal for Your house has eaten
> me up...
>
> — Psalm 69:9 NKJV

A fire is lit inside of you, and everything changes. The Holy Spirit begins shaping you—constantly transforming you into the image of Christ.

It may sound radical, but it's true: Your faith life means nothing without the Holy Spirit. Your prayer life is powerless without Him. Your worship, without His presence, is merely a sound. God is seeking true worshipers—those who worship Him in spirit and in truth—and that's only possible through the Holy Spirit. This is the precious gift that sets the church of Jesus Christ apart from the world: the indwelling presence of the Spirit of God.

The Holy Spirit came in the form of a dove. With the utmost reverence, I often say the dove is like a logo of what God is doing. If you study a dove, you'll notice something symbolic: It has nine feathers on its right wing and nine on its left. The right wing symbolizes the nine gifts of the Spirit, and the left wing represents the nine fruits of the Spirit. The main tail feather of a dove consists of five feathers, representing the fivefold ministry—apostle, prophet, evangelist, pastor, and teacher. Remarkably, the dove is also one of the few animals without a gallbladder, signifying purity and the absence of deceit.

This image isn't just poetic—it's prophetic. The Holy Spirit comes not to flutter by, but to remain. He brings gifts, fruit, order, purity, and power. He doesn't just touch you for a moment; He wants to dwell, transform, and ignite you with holy fire.

Doves mate for life. He will be with you until the very end of the Earth. When Jesus came and was baptized, He came to demonstrate something powerful. What He was saying is this: After the anointing of the Holy Spirit, He would release the nine gifts the church would need. He would also release the nine fruits, because while the gifts are proof that God can use a man, the fruits are evidence that the man has been with God. He would empower the fivefold ministry, and since no deceit is found in Him, the Holy Spirit is rightly called the Spirit of truth.

Now, when you watch the news or listen to the world and something inside of you says, "That's not right," understand—it's not a something, it's a Someone. The Holy Spirit leads you into all truth. Just because everyone is doing something doesn't make it the truth. You'll have to know Him. You will know the truth, and the truth shall set you free (John 8:32).

If I see a dove on the street and suddenly approach it, it flies away. If one were to rest on my shoulder, and I jumped up without thinking, the dove would flee. If I want the dove to remain, I have to move carefully. I must consider the dove. I can no longer do as I please. I need to know Him—what He loves, what He hates. My life is no longer about me. It's about Him. I have to consider His ways and not grieve Him.

This is what lovers of the Holy Spirit do. We consider Him. We don't go to bed the same way we used to. We don't watch what we used to watch. We don't speak the way we used to speak. Why? Because we want to keep Him close. We want to please Him. We don't want to hurt Him. We must consider the dove. We must consider the Holy Spirit if we want Him to remain upon us. He will never lead us into unrighteousness; He will always lead us to truth.

It's time for the Body of Christ to consider our ways. I don't just get up and make my own decisions anymore—I must ask myself, "Does this bring Him glory?" "Will this grieve the Holy Spirit?" I believe that even now, the Holy Spirit is doing deep work in many hearts. It is only at Jesus' baptism that the Holy Spirit was described as a dove, because Jesus was saying, "Now this is what I will do for My body. I am releasing the nine gifts, the nine fruits, the fivefold ministry—and this is the sign that the Holy Spirit can remain."

Let me make a bold statement: If you are not closer to God today than you were yesterday, then you've started to grow cold. You haven't considered the Holy Spirit lately. After this moment of baptism and empowerment, Jesus said to His followers, "You will heal the sick, cleanse the lepers, and raise the dead—but wait until you are endowed with power from on high" (Matthew 10:8 and

Luke 24:49). If you go now without this power, you will make a mess of it. You need that *dunamis* power that Jesus Himself walked in.

If you want to do what Jesus did, you must have what Jesus had. You can't fulfill your calling without Him. You can't do it outside of Him. We must consider the Holy Spirit now more than ever before. Jesus said, "You will receive power after the Holy Spirit has come upon you" (Acts 1:8). After—not before.

The Holy Spirit comes after the relationship—after the seeking, after the yielding. That's why Paul says, "And do not grieve the Holy Spirit" (Ephesians 4:30). Do you know what that word *grieve* really means? It means: Do not hurt Him deeply by the way that you live. Let me say it again until it becomes a revelation—do not hurt Him deeply by the way that you live. Many people grieve the Holy Spirit every day, not through words, but through lifestyle. And yet, He remains gentle.

Here's something you must understand about the Holy Spirit: He never puts the spotlight on Himself, and He never places the spotlight on any other personality besides Jesus Christ. I believe in the fivefold ministry, and I honor it. But when someone operating in one of those offices walks into the room, the Holy Spirit will not draw attention to the apostle, or the prophet, or the evangelist, or the pastor, or the teacher. He will only draw attention to Jesus. This is how you know whether a person is truly of God—because the Holy Spirit will always return the glory to Jesus. He will help you magnify the Lord. He will always lead you to Him.

Jesus said, "It is better if I go, because if I do not go, I cannot send the Helper" (John 16:7). Think about that for a moment. He loved the Holy Spirit so much that He said, "I will pray to the Father to send Him" (John 14:16). The Father loves the Holy Spirit so deeply that even Jesus said, "I will ask Him." And then Jesus said this: "When the Spirit of truth comes, the world will not receive Him, because it neither sees Him nor knows Him. But you will know Him, for He will be with you and He will be in you" (John 14:17).

## Chapter 9

### The Mysteries of the Holy Spirit

I call this *The Mysteries of the Holy Spirit* because many people don't understand that life with the Spirit is a life of power. Outside of the Holy Spirit, there is no power. You can have all the knowledge in the world, but knowledge alone only puffs up the individual.

**Think about this:** We all have saliva in our mouths, and saliva is a good thing. The gastric juices in your stomach are also good. If you eat without saliva, that hamburger is going to get stuck in your esophagus—and you're going to choke. Saliva softens and prepares the food, and then the gastric juices break it down. Some of what you eat is burned off as energy, and some becomes fat. I see it this way: The Word of God without the Holy Spirit is like eating dry food without saliva. It just gets stuck and never becomes anything useful. That's why Paul said:

> And my speech and my preaching were not with persuasive words of human wisdom, but in demonstration of the Spirit and of power, that your faith should not be in the wisdom of men but in the power of God.
>
> — 1 CORINTHIANS 2:4–5 (NKJV)

Paul was saying, "When I came to you, I didn't impress you with eloquent words or lofty speech." He wasn't the best speaker—but he was a great demonstrator. Yet today, we've replaced that. Many churches have exchanged the supernatural power of God for feel-good messages. We've traded fivefold ministers for public speakers and motivational personalities. But Paul says the opposite. He declares that the Kingdom of God is not in word only, but in power.

You can quote Scripture all day long and say, "The Lord is my Shepherd," but until the Holy Spirit breathes *rhema*[i] into that verse—until He makes it come alive in your heart—it remains just ink on paper. That's why we need both the Word and the Holy Ghost.

Paul didn't want anyone's faith to rest in human wisdom. He said, "I came with the demonstration of the Spirit and of power, so your faith wouldn't be in man—but in the power of God." The gospel must be preached *and* demonstrated with power.

The world needs to see that power. I remember a woman in Kentucky, eighty years old, who came to one of my meetings with a broken back in two places. When I prayed for her, the power of God rushed through her body—and her back was instantly healed. Another time, a precious woman in one of my meetings was blind in one eye and needed a brand-new retina. As I laid hands on her, God performed a creative miracle. Her blind eye opened.

When the Holy Spirit became my best friend, the frequency of miracles increased dramatically in my life. I remember ministering in Ethiopia, where thousands gathered at a conference. A woman brought her two-year-old son, who could not walk. She placed him at the base of the stage and told me she wasn't a Christian, but she wanted to see if my God heals or kills.

We had a medical doctor on site to verify the miracles. I laid my hands on the child, and I felt the power of the Holy Spirit move through his body. We picked him up, and he began to walk—by the power of God! That mother fell to her knees and gave her life to Jesus Christ.

Hallelujah! What a Savior we serve. A Savior who heals. A God who empowers His people through the person of the Holy Spirit.

I was in Cape Town, South Africa, when I met a man in a wheelchair—completely paralyzed from the neck down. The doctors had told him he would never walk again. But as I stood there with him, I felt the power from Heaven begin to fill the room. I laid my hands on him and prayed. Suddenly, he began to stand up. Then he started walking. Jesus healed him!

After God created man in Genesis, man was still just a lifeless form—until God breathed into his nostrils, and man became a living being. That breath was the Holy Spirit, the One in charge of manifestation.

The Bible says the Spirit of God hovered over the face of the deep, and then God said, "Let there be light" (Genesis 1:3). Notice the sequence—the Spirit moved, *then* the Word was released. That is how it still works. The Holy Spirit prepares the atmosphere, sets the stage, and releases power when the Word is spoken.

Understand this: The Holy Spirit is not a dove. He is not a fire. He is not an atmosphere. He is the One *who brings* the atmosphere of Heaven. He is a fire-bringer. He is a Creator. When He touches someone with cancer, that cancer dries up—because the power of creation flows through Him. Wherever He moves, the impossible becomes possible.

Today, more than ever, the church needs the Holy Spirit. Without Him, we are just a social club, a gathering without power. We don't need more people to be "woke"—we need people to be filled to overflowing with the Holy Ghost. That will change you. That will set you apart.

I was once invited to speak at a large church in South Africa—eight hours away by car. A week before the trip, the Lord told me, "I want you to preach on the Holy Spirit." I said, "Yes, Lord." But when I arrived, the pastor shook my hand and said, "Thank you for coming. My house is your house. Preach whatever you like…except on the Holy Spirit."

He looked me in the eyes and said, "The Holy Spirit is dead. If you preach on Him, I will remove you publicly."

I turned to the Lord in my heart and asked, "What do I do? You told me to preach on the Holy Spirit, and now this man forbids it." And I heard the Lord say, "Who do you fear?" I answered, "Lord, I fear You." He said, "Then preach what I told you to preach." "Yes, Lord."

That day, the pastor opened the service and began denouncing the Holy Spirit from the pulpit. He said, "This church does not allow any preaching on the Holy Spirit. He is dead." Then he introduced me, not knowing what message I was carrying.

I stepped to the pulpit, trying to remain composed, but the first words out of my mouth were, "Church, the Holy Spirit is more alive than this pastor."

The room shifted. The pastor—seated three rows from the front—became visibly angry. His expression changed. You could see the fire in his eyes. He began standing up, then sitting down. Then he suddenly jumped from his seat as if it were on fire and rushed toward me.

I turned to him and declared, "In the name of Jesus!"

The fire of God hit him, and he collapsed under the power of God. His ushers rushed forward to help him, but the moment they touched him, they also fell to the ground. God kept them there the entire service. That day, people were healed, filled with the Holy Spirit, and delivered.

That church no longer exists—but the move of the Spirit that day changed lives forever.

The Holy Spirit helps us live the Christian life. He makes Jesus real to us. He makes our worship acceptable. He brings the very atmosphere of Heaven. He helps us in our weakness. He takes us from timidity to boldness. He is the power of Heaven living inside of us.

When we don't know how to pray, *He* prays through us. He brings revelation as we read the Word. He is *holy* and worthy of our worship, our devotion, and our affection.

He is called the Set-Apart Spirit—and we are called to be a set-apart people, housing the glory of God daily. What an honor it is to know Him, to love Him, and to carry His presence within us.

## Chapter 10

### Three Ways the Holy Spirit Comes

There are three ways the Holy Spirit comes into a believer's life.

### He comes to be with you.

The Holy Spirit comes to be *with* you—to lead you, to guide you, to help you, and to protect you.

You've probably heard the Scripture: *"When the enemy comes in like a flood, the Spirit of the Lord will lift up a standard against him."* But did you know the original Hebrew text had no punctuation? That means the verse should more accurately read: *"When the enemy comes, like a flood, the Holy Spirit will raise up a standard against him"* (Isaiah 59:19).

Satan cannot come like a flood—but the Holy Spirit can. The Holy Ghost comes like a flood! The Devil wants you to believe he has overwhelming power, but he doesn't. The Bible says he's *under our feet*. In the Garden of Eden, God told the serpent, "You will be lower than the cattle" (Genesis 3:14). Let that sink in—are you afraid of a devil who has less authority than a cow?

Now think about *where you are.* You're seated with Christ in heavenly places. All authority, dominion, and power have been given to the Church. Jesus didn't give that power to Gabriel or Michael. He gave it to us—His body, the Church.

Jesus told Peter:

> And I also say to you that you are Peter, and on this rock I will build My church, and the gates of Hades shall not prevail against it. And I will give you the keys of the kingdom of heaven, and whatever you bind on earth will be bound in heaven, and whatever you loose on earth will be loosed in heaven.
>
> — MATTHEW 16:18-19 NKJV

So, where is the Church today? It's time we rise up in our authority. It's time to tell the Devil, *"Someone's moving today—and it's not me!"*

You've got *dunamis* power inside you. The Holy Spirit is not "something"—He is *someone*. He is the one who whispers, "Don't go there." He is the one who shields you, leads you, and helps you.

Scripture tells us the Spirit of God *yearns jealously* over you (James 4:5). He is a jealous God—not in the way the world defines jealousy, but with a holy desire for your full affection, your full attention, and your obedience.

The Holy Spirit doesn't come to play games. He comes to establish truth, to bring power, and to protect the body of Christ. He is with you—every step of the way.

### He comes to be in you.

The Bible teaches that the Holy Spirit not only comes to be *with* you—leading, guiding, and protecting—but He also comes to dwell *in* you. Jesus said, "And He will be in you" (John 14:17). Why does He come *in* you? One-word answer: sanctification.

It is impossible to live a holy life without the Holy Spirit. When someone gives their life to Jesus, they often think, 'Now I can't do this, and I can't do that.' But when the Holy Spirit comes, it's no longer, *"I can't,"* it becomes, *"I don't want to."* Why? Because the Holy Spirit changes you from the inside out. He transforms your desires. He makes you want what is holy.

His main job is to shape you into the image of the Son. You begin to hate the things of this world. You hate sin.

You may lose friends. Family may stop calling. They might even think you're strange. But it's not you—it's the Spirit of God in you that the demons in them can't stand. That's why they treat you differently. And that's okay. It's actually a good thing. It's a sign that God's hand is on your life.

The Holy Spirit is the one who brings holiness. The Bible says He convicts the world of sin, of righteousness, and of judgment (John 16:8).

When sinners feel offended in church, it's not the pastor's words that upset them—it's their *sin*. Light and darkness cannot coexist (2 Corinthians 6:14). When light shows up, darkness rises to the surface. People might say, "That sermon hurt my feelings," but it's not the preacher—it's the Holy Spirit trying to say, "There's a better way. You don't have to die in your sin. Let Me change you."

Now, once you are in Christ, the Holy Spirit no longer convicts you of sin in the same way. Instead, He convicts you of righteousness. He constantly reminds you who you are in God.

He whispers, "Don't respond in anger. You're better than that. Don't go there. You belong to Jesus. You're set apart. You're My vessel." The Holy Spirit convinces you—He confirms your identity. He reminds you daily that you are a child of God.

HE COMES UPON YOU.

> "But you shall receive power when the
> Holy Spirit has come upon you;
> and you shall be witnesses to Me in
> Jerusalem, and in all Judea
> and Samaria, and to the end of the
> earth."
>
> — ACTS 1:8 NKJV

The third way the Holy Spirit comes is *upon you*—for power, boldness, and demonstration. Acts 1:8 says clearly that power comes *after* the Holy Spirit comes *upon* you.

The Bible tells us that the believers gathered in the upper room in *one accord.* They didn't have distractions. They weren't divided. Scripture says all 120 were praying, seeking, and waiting. And all 120 received. Why? Because all 120 were desperate to be changed. They were hungry.

These weren't random people. These were the same disciples who had once said, "We'll die with Him," but who scattered in fear when the pressure came. They saw Jesus heal the sick, raise the dead, cast out demons, and calm the storm. He taught them everything. But still, they lacked the courage to stand. It wasn't until the Holy Spirit *came upon them* that they turned the world upside down.

When God created Adam, the Bible says He formed man from the dust—but man was lifeless. It wasn't until God *breathed* into his nostrils that man became a living being (Genesis 2:7). That breath was the Holy Spirit.

Have you ever thought about the name *Yahweh*? In ancient Hebrew manuscripts, the name of God was often considered so holy that they would leave it blank. But when you try to pronounce *Yahweh* correctly, without moving your tongue, it sounds like a breath:

YAHHH…weh.

That's the breath of God. From the moment of your first breath, you're declaring His name. Even an atheist, breathing their last, will unconsciously call out, *Yahweh*. That's how deeply God has woven His Spirit into our very being.

So, if you're facing disease or despair, remember this: You still have the breath of God in you. Before cancer, there was the Word. Before high blood pressure, HIV, or diabetes, there was the Word. And *in the beginning was the Word, and the Word was with God, and the Word was God* (John 1:1). The Word has the final say—not the diagnosis.

The moment the Holy Spirit came upon Peter, the Bible says the place was *shaken* by the power of God. That's what happens when He comes *upon* you—not just *with* you or *in* you, but *upon* you.

This is the power that emboldens believers, heals the sick, casts out demons, and transforms ordinary men and women into Kingdom warriors. Without the Holy Spirit upon you, ministry is dry. But with Him, it is alive, powerful, and fruitful.

Let the breath of God fill you again. Let Him come upon you—not just for your sake, but for the world that needs to see that Jesus is alive.

## CHAPTER 11

### SUDDENLY, EVERYTHING CHANGES

The early believers came together in one accord. Every time you want to see God move, you must be in one accord. There must be unity of heart and mind around one purpose: we need a move of God's Spirit. Where are the people who say, "I'm not leaving this place the same way I came, in Jesus' name"? That's what happened in the upper room—they came together with one mind, and the Bible says they prayed (Acts 1:14). They didn't do anything else. They didn't strategize or organize—they *prayed*. And they were waiting on the promise.

They didn't even fully understand what the promise would look like, but they waited. Today, people don't want to wait. But if you want the Holy Spirit to show up in power, you'll have to *wait*. I've said this my whole life: so often we say, "We're just waiting on God," but the truth is, God is waiting on us. What we really mean is that God is waiting until the last bit of our flesh dies, so He can release His power into surrendered vessels.

God wants to reveal Himself to you—but His presence always comes with the absence of self. Flesh has to die for the Spirit to move. That's the pattern. That's the price.

They came together praying, waiting, and then—suddenly. The Bible says, "And suddenly..." When the Holy Spirit shows up, He doesn't trickle in. He doesn't arrive gradually. He comes suddenly—and when He comes, everything changes.

I believe God is about to do some *suddenlies* in your life that will blow your mind. Sudden healings. Sudden provision. Sudden restoration. Sudden breakthrough. A *suddenly* that will take you further than you could have gone in ten years on your own. Suddenly, the things that were stuck will start to move. Suddenly, there's a door that no man can shut. Suddenly, what looked dead will be resurrected.

Let me say this again: God is going to do something suddenly. Suddenly, you'll be pregnant. Suddenly, your child will come home. Suddenly, your mind will be clear. Suddenly, your addiction is broken. Suddenly, there's favor you can't explain. Why? Because when the Holy Spirit shows up, He moves in power—and He moves suddenly.

I've learned something walking with the Holy Spirit. When He first came in Acts 2, He came suddenly—and with a sound. The Bible says, "Suddenly there came a *sound* from heaven..." (Acts 2:2). That's because the Kingdom of God moves through *sound*. It's why we worship. It's why we sing. It's why we cry out in faith.

Bartimaeus cried out, "Son of David, have mercy on me!" (Mark 10:47-48). He didn't whisper it. He shouted. And when he released that sound, Jesus stopped. When your sound matches your desperation, Heaven responds.

If you have a *sound* inside of you that you're willing to release, I believe with all my heart that the Holy Spirit will show up suddenly. And when He does, everything changes.

Suddenly, there came a sound from Heaven as of a mighty rushing wind—a mighty wind. The Bible says it filled the whole house where the disciples were waiting. And then, upon each of them appeared divided tongues of fire (Acts 2:2-3). Why *divided* tongues of fire? Because there were two tongues upon each head. One tongue represents God's tongue. The second tongue represents your tongue. God was declaring in that moment: "The words in My mouth are now the same as the words of My Spirit in your mouth."

Suddenly, the place was shaken by the power of God, and they began to speak in other tongues as the Spirit gave them utterance (Acts 2:4). The people outside looked on and said, "These men are drunk" (Acts 2:13). But Peter stood up and declared, "We are not drunk, as you suppose. This is that." What is *that*? It is the fulfillment of what the prophet Joel declared: "In the last days, says God, I will pour out My Spirit upon all flesh" (Acts 2:14-17).

## Miracle of the Rotting Leg

In one of my meetings, a man came forward who had been scheduled for leg amputation. His bone was so rotten that even metal rods couldn't hold it together. They had already measured him for a prosthetic. I laid my hands on his leg and declared a creative miracle in Jesus' name.

When he went back to the doctor on the day of the scheduled amputation, three different doctors examined him. All three confirmed: his bone was completely restored. There was no need for amputation. Not only did God heal his leg, but He also restored his finances. That's the kind of overflow our God works in.

## Miracle in the Philippines

Another man in the Philippines was diagnosed with stage 4 cancer. He had been sent home to die. But he came to my meeting and sat in the front row. During the message, he said that spit from my mouth accidentally landed in his mouth.

You know what he said? "It didn't bother me because I knew you were a man of God."

Later, the doctors examined him and confirmed that his cancer was completely gone. He was healed by the spit that carried the anointing of God. Why? Because when the Holy Spirit anoints you, He anoints everything about you—your words, your breath, your presence, even the unexpected things like spit.

Suddenly, everything changed.

## Chapter 12

### He Is a Person, Not an It

The Holy Spirit is not a force or a feeling—He is a person. He makes decisions. He feels. He leads. He speaks. But the problem is, many people still see Him as an "it." Think about a pulpit—it's an object. I can use it to hold my Bible, or I could even throw it at someone if I wanted to. But the pulpit cannot use me. It's an object. As long as you see the Holy Spirit as an "it," you'll keep trying to use Him. But the moment you recognize Him as a Person, you will allow Him to use you. He is not to be manipulated—He is to be worshiped, obeyed, and followed.

Many people think that when the Holy Spirit comes, it's just a feeling or an atmosphere. Do you know why the atmosphere changes? Because the very atmosphere of Heaven steps into a place. The creation of Heaven enters the room. It's not goosebumps—it's a Person. Expect the Person to walk into the room. "Where do you get that from?" you might ask. God said in the beginning, "Let Us make man in Our image, after Our likeness" (Genesis 1:26). He wasn't speaking to Gabriel. He wasn't speaking to the angels. I'm not made in the image of an angel. I've been created in the image of God.

When I say the name Jesus, most people immediately picture Jesus—brown hair, brown beard. But when I say Holy Spirit, for many, it's a mystery. They have no mental image. Let me tell you: the Holy Spirit has a face. He has eyes. He has a mouth. He has ears. He has hands. He is an extremely intelligent Being. He is God Almighty. I like to call Him "Jesus Unlimited." When Jesus walked the Earth, He was limited to one place and one time. But the Holy Spirit is unlimited. While He's moving here, He's also moving in Miami, Houston, Johannesburg—everywhere at once.

What I believe with all of my heart is that the church must come back to that place of genuine hunger, the place where we seek God with everything in us. Where we say, "Holy Spirit, I'm not leaving until You touch me." I believe He is yearning for people who will say, "Here I am. I can't do this without You."

## Chapter 13

### Obedience and Intimacy

I'd returned home after preaching for two weeks, and my life changed. I was completely exhausted. I sat down on my couch late at night and thought, 'I'm going to have a soda, and then I'm going to bed.' But I heard God speak to me: "I want you to go and pray." I said, "Lord, I promise You—I'll pray tomorrow. I'm just so tired right now. Please let me sleep." A few minutes passed, and I heard Him again: "I want you to pray." That pulled me to the edge of my seat. I said, "Lord, I love You, but I've explained—I'm exhausted. You know my heart. Tomorrow, I'll pray." Then I heard Him a third time: "Wessel, pray lest My Spirit withdraws from you." That got my attention. I jumped up, ran to my prayer room, and closed the door. As soon as I did, I fell to my knees—there was no time to say a word—He was already there. I fell on my face and wept for at least an hour. The floor was covered in puddles of tears. The holiness of

God was in that room. I couldn't look up; I felt that if I dared lift my face, I would die.

After about an hour, I came out, sat on the couch, and tried to figure out what had just happened. Then I heard Him again: "Go back." I went back, closed the door, and the same thing happened. I fell on my face and wept before the Lord. I couldn't even get words out—just tears in His glory. When I came out again, I headed to the kitchen and switched on the kettle. Then I heard Him say something that rocked me to my core: "Wessel, I loved spending time with you. Would you spend a few more minutes?" I thought, 'Who am I that God would say He loves spending time with me?' I ran back to that room and fell on my face again. This time, I heard Him say, "Whatever you ask Me now, I'll give it to you." I had a list. I thought, 'Here we go—I've got needs, and here's the list.' But the only thing that came out of my mouth was, "Lord, I want more of You. If this is it, I want more of You."

That night, I realized He's jealous over our time. I realized that if I want the Holy Spirit to stay, I must obey when He knocks. I asked the Lord, "Please never speak to me three times about something. Help me to obey You the first time. If You knock on my heart once to pray, I want to pray."

He's a real person—with real feelings. I believe the Holy Spirit is the most offended Person in the church today. He's often left outside while the church continues without Him. But we cannot do this without Him. He is the precious gift from God who quickens us, changes us, and takes our prayer life and makes it powerful.

Think about this: The Bible says that no angel knows the depths of the Father's heart. No angel knows the secrets of God. Only the Holy Spirit does—and He reveals them to us, the heirs of salvation. In other words, the Holy Spirit reveals what's inside the heart of God (1 Corinthians 2:10-11). No angel can do that. Angels surround the throne of God day and night, crying out: "Holy, holy, holy is the Lord God Almighty" (Revelation 4:8).

But what does that even mean? Every time an angel cries "Holy," they're trying to sum up the entirety of who God is in one word—*Holy*. When I say *Holy*, I'm saying: wonderful, glorious, righteous, victorious, triumphant, healer, deliverer, shield, defender, strong tower, my best friend, omnipotent, omnipresent, soon and coming King, Alpha, Omega, Lord of everything, Lion of the tribe of Judah, the Rock of my salvation, the Captain of our faith...and I'm wrapping all of that up in one single word—*Holy*.

Angels will do that for all eternity. Why? Because every time they say *Holy*, they encounter a new dimension of God's heart. Every cry is born from a fresh revelation. For all of eternity, they'll continue discovering new depths of who He is.

But here's the truly amazing part: *We*—the heirs of salvation—have the Holy Spirit living in us. He doesn't just give us glimpses from the outside like the angels; He makes the Father *real* to us from the inside. He is the one who reveals Jesus, who shows us the heart of the Father, and who speaks the secrets of God to our spirit. That's what makes Him so personal, so intimate, and so life-transforming.

He's the one who takes a broken life and turns it around—who says, "Come back, son. Come back, daughter. Just as you are." He's the one who mends hearts. Scripture says He is near to the brokenhearted, close to the one with a crushed spirit (Psalm 34:18). I've seen it time and again—people who were on the edge of suicide, encountering the Holy Spirit, and being changed forever. He's the one who turns Sauls into Pauls. One encounter with Him will take a Simon and turn him into a Peter. Just imagine what an encounter with the Holy Spirit can do for your life!

# Chapter 14

## Natural vs. Spiritual Man

Where's your biggest devil? Let me tell you—the only authority the Devil has over you is the authority *you* give him.

When he comes whispering lies, you need to respond with boldness and truth: "Devil, let me remind you of who you are. You were cast out of Heaven. All your authority has been stripped away. You've been made a public spectacle. Jesus triumphed over you at the cross. The blood of Jesus is against you, and you are under my feet."

When the Devil says, "You're going to die young," you'd better jump to your feet and respond: "Devil, the Bible says you are the father of lies (John 8:44). My God said, 'With long life I will satisfy you' (Psalm 91:16). I declare right now—I will not die young. I will live and declare the works of the Lord."

The Devil does not hold the power of life and death—you do. The Bible says life and death are in the power of the tongue. That's why I *prophesy*:

- I will live long.
- I will walk in divine health.
- I will flourish in God's abundance.
- Because greater is He who is in me than he who is in the world.

Say it out loud: I've got Holy Ghost power!

You are not powerless. You're not defeated. You're about to receive a heavenly deposit—a supernatural endowment from on high that will hit you with *joy unspeakable and full of glory*.

Get ready. Victory is your portion. The blood has already won it.

## Chapter 15

### Living with Power and Joy

Let me tell you what *joy* really means.

Joy means that even in the face of adversity, you can declare: "My God is a good God."

Even though you walk through the valley of the shadow of death, you fear no evil—because you know who walks with you. You can stare death in the face and *laugh at the Devil*, saying: "Death has been conquered. I've got joy unspeakable and full of glory."

The Apostle Paul, locked in prison, wrote to the church: "Rejoice in the Lord always" (Philippians 4:4).

Here's a man in chains, encouraging others to find their joy. Why? Because joy doesn't come from your surroundings—joy flows from the overflow of Jesus in your heart.

The first thing the Holy Spirit taught Jesus in the wilderness wasn't how to preach or how to build a crowd. It was how to *whip the Devil.*

When Satan showed up, Jesus said, "It is written" (Matthew 4:3-10). That was the weapon. The Word of God in the mouth of the Son of God.

Likewise, the first lesson the Holy Spirit wants to teach every believer is how to put the enemy in his place. But instead, we've got too many believers walking around saying, "I don't know what I'm going to do." And the Devil *laughs.*

But when the Holy Spirit gets hold of a man, that man stands toe to toe with Hell and says: "You picked the wrong person. You picked the wrong family. Let me tell you who I am. I'm blood-washed. I'm Spirit-filled. I'm a fire-breather. I've got resurrection power living on the inside of me. And Devil—if I open my mouth—you're finished!" That's the joy and power of the Holy Ghost.

If the Holy Spirit had to teach Jesus how to handle the Devil's attacks, how much more must the Church of Jesus Christ understand how to fight back against this wicked thing?

The Bible tells us that at the end of the age, the world will look at the Devil and say in shock: "Is this the one who made the earth tremble? This thing?" (Isaiah 14:16). They will be stunned. People will realize they spent their lives being tormented by something so *small*—so *defeated.*

We've been conditioned to tie our joy to our circumstances. If things are good, we're happy. If things go wrong, we're sad. But that's not *real joy*. That's an emotional reaction.

Supernatural joy is when, in the midst of adversity, you declare: "My God is good. I don't know how He's going to do it—but that's not my business. I just know I'm coming out of this." You don't need to figure out the "how." Your job is to *believe*.

"All things work together for the good of those who love God and are called according to His purpose" (Romans 8:28). If you're a lover of God, then hear this: Whatever the enemy meant for evil, God is turning it for your good.

**Say it boldly: "Everything is going to be okay."**

Why? Because greater is He that is in me than any diagnosis, any disaster, or any Devil.

Even in death, the enemy doesn't win. If a child of God dies and the doctor writes out a death certificate, there is no loss. You cannot stand at that coffin and say the Devil won—he didn't. "O death, where is your sting?" (1 Corinthians 15:55).

Paul said, "Whether I live or die, I win either way. It's gain" (Philippians 1:21). That's victory. That's joy. That's the power of the Holy Spirit living on the inside.

As long as I'm alive, then I'm going to live boldly. I'm going to serve God faithfully. And if I die? Then I'll be with Jesus for all eternity. Either way—I win. Nothing can block me from His mighty hand. Nothing can stop what God has already begun. I've got God Himself living on the inside of me!

Paul said:

> And my language and my message were not set forth in persuasive (enticing and plausible) words of wisdom, but they were in demonstration of the [Holy] Spirit and power [a proof by the Spirit and power of God, operating on me and stirring in the minds of my hearers the most holy emotions and thus persuading them], So that your faith might not rest in the wisdom of men (human philosophy), but in the power of God.
>
> — 1 Corinthians 2:4–5 AMPC

That's how I preach. That's how I live. Not with persuasive words—but with a demonstration of power. Demonstration is not always about people falling down. Real demonstration is this—you came in one way, but you walk out changed. You leave with greater faith. You know who's living on the inside of you. You walk into next week stronger than you've ever been.

**Say it: "I've got power living inside of me."**

> "...because greater is he that is in you,
> than he that is in the world."
>
> — 1 John 4:4 KJV

Jesus breathed on the disciples and said, "Receive the Holy Spirit" (John 20:22). He gave them authority and power. This wasn't Acts 2 yet—this was personal impartation. Authority by breath. And when the Holy Spirit comes upon you, things begin to *move*. You get turned inside out. People around you won't recognize you. They'll say, "Who is this guy? He's different." That's what revival looks like.

"Oh, what a change. I've got Jesus on the inside, working on the outside, bringing about a change in my life." Are you thankful that He changed you?

After salvation, the Holy Spirit doesn't just visit—He stays. When I leave the church building, He comes with me. If I walk into a dark, godless environment, I bring the answer. Why? Because God walks in with me.

I'm so connected with Him that when I move, He moves. When I stretch out my hand, He stretches out His. When I speak, He speaks through me. The Spirit of God has taken permanent residency in my life.

**Say it: "I am changed."**

That essential Person you need to be a Christian lives in you now.

What happens when the Holy Spirit takes up residence in a man? The first thing He changes is your nature. That's what many people don't understand. They think salvation is just a prayer. But Scripture calls the Holy Spirit "the Spirit of grace." When you were born again, the Spirit of grace came to live inside you—not just to comfort you, but to transform you. The Bible says He was given as a guarantee of our salvation. That means He seals you, marks you, and begins the work of total transformation.

Suddenly, the things you used to crave no longer satisfy you. Your spouse doesn't need to beg you to stop drinking. The desire is just *gone*. When your old friends call to ask, "Are we clubbing tonight?" you can say, "Yeah—I'm clubbing at the altar on Sunday morning. That's my kind of club now. I'm in the Trinity Club. I'm drinking that Holy Ghost wine. I'm getting filled up all over again!"

Because joy isn't based on your past—it's based on Jesus' triumph. Hell is defeated. The grave is conquered. The curse is broken. The Devil has no more power. So now, I've got joy in the Holy Ghost.

Are you ready for that kind of joy?

> ...for the joy of the Lord is your strength.
>
> — Nehemiah 8:10 KJV

Lord, let every person reading this come to understand—by Your Spirit—that the Greater One lives inside of them. Not only to make them conquerors, but to make them more than conquerors. Thank You, Lord, that we know what's going on in this world can only be overcome through the power of the supernatural—and that through the Holy Spirit in us, every wicked scheme can be broken and every darkness can bow its knees.

Thank You that the same Spirit who raised Jesus from the dead is now living in us, bringing the atmosphere of Heaven everywhere we go—changing our character, reshaping our nature, and making us like Christ.

So let's make a bold declaration together:

"Today, I'm going to do serious business with Heaven. I've got joy unspeakable and full of glory!"

## Chapter 16

### Holy Spirit, My Best Friend

The reason you're here today is because somewhere along the line, the Holy Spirit fought for you. Hell wanted you, but the Holy Spirit said, "Not on my watch." Most people imagine the Holy Spirit as some gentle old dove floating in a church window, but I'm telling you—there's a fighter living inside of you. There's a dreamer, a visionary, a warrior. The reason you have dreams is because He's dreaming through you. The reason you have vision is because He's seeing through you.

Have you ever found yourself just sitting and thinking, 'This is the dream I want to accomplish'? That's not random. That's the Holy Spirit waking it up inside of you. He's the dreamer, and He is stirring your spirit again.

> So [as the result of the Messiah's intervention] they shall [reverently] fear the name of the Lord from the west, and His glory from the rising of the sun. When the enemy shall come in like a flood, the Spirit of the Lord will lift up a standard against him...
>
> — Isaiah 59:19 (AMPC)

He's aggressive in your defense.

People walk around repeating what the Devil told them. *"The Devil said this... the Devil said that..."* No. I am hidden in Christ, and Satan has no access. He's not my equal. He's not my adversary. He's under my feet. I don't have to fight him—he's already defeated. Jesus stripped Satan and made an open spectacle of him on the cross. The blood of Jesus speaks louder.

When I don't know what to pray, I pray in the Holy Ghost. I stir up my most holy faith. And suddenly, the Holy Spirit surrounds me like a wall and says, "Get behind me, Satan."

I've been talking about the power of my best friend, and I'm telling you, you can have that same power today. Suddenly, everything shifts. Suddenly, fear is replaced with faith. Suddenly, your life is flipped upside down—in the best way.

The Bible says Peter walked the streets, and people laid the sick in his shadow, and they were healed (Acts 5:15). What kind of power must be present for a man's shadow to carry the healing of Heaven? That's the power of the Holy Spirit. That's the intimacy we've been called into.

But sadly, many Christians today wouldn't even notice if the Holy Spirit left their lives. They would keep going through the motions. Why? Because we've lost our regard for the Holy Spirit. We cater to every fleshly desire, but when it comes to the Spirit, we make excuses. We'll go cycling on Sunday, chase after the world all week, and then cry about the crime and corruption. But the Holy Spirit is still being ignored, still standing outside the door—waiting to be invited back in.

Many Christians believe they have God's presence in them and on them, yet they live an empty life—a life of noise but no impact—no real change. I struggle to understand how Christians can live depressed, defeated, or oppressed. I don't get it—because we have the same Spirit that raised Jesus from the dead living inside of us. Not a copy, not a lesser version—the same Spirit that crushed death, Hell, and the grave. The same Spirit that anointed Jesus Christ of Nazareth and unleashed signs and wonders. The same Spirit that hit the early Church and turned the world upside down now lives inside you and me.

That means there's no room for despondency, no excuse for intimidation, depression, or brokenness because God lives inside of you. The indwelling Holy Spirit is not a feeling—it's your source of constant victory. You don't have to live one day on the mountaintop and the next day in the valley. With Him, it's glory to glory, and strength to strength. He is always lifting you, transforming you, and empowering you. I'm going from glory to glory.

> But the natural [unbelieving] man does not accept the things [the teachings and revelations] of the Spirit of God, for they are foolishness [absurd and illogical] to him...
>
> — 1 Corinthians 2:14 (AMP)

The natural man can't receive anything from God—it's all foolishness to him. He cannot discern the things of the Spirit. And that's the difference. I'm not writing to natural people—I'm writing this to the spiritual ones. The ones who say, "I want to go higher. I want to live Spirit-led." Natural people can't take you where God wants to lead you. They'll look at your life and say, "This doesn't make sense. This doesn't add up." They'll look at your spreadsheet and say, "There's no way this is possible." But the spiritual man knows better: "As long as I'm filled with the Holy Ghost, nothing is impossible for me."

*"Well, Wessel, I don't understand those people who fall over in church."* Of course, you don't—because you're trying to understand spiritual things with a natural mind. But let me tell you something: In the book of Acts, the Holy Ghost fell on them—bam! Jesus stood in Gethsemane and said, "Who are you looking for?" They answered, "Jesus." He said, "I AM." And they fell backward (John 18:4-6). What was He saying? "Let Me show you—I'm still in control." When they hit the ground, He was letting them know, "You're not taking Me. I'm giving Myself freely. I'm still in charge."

The natural man fights spiritual things. He can't understand them. He might understand religion. He might understand logic. But he has no clue what it means to be Spirit-filled. But the mature believer—the spiritual man—discerns. He sees. He knows. He doesn't bow to what's illogical. He says, *"I'm in an illogical situation, but I serve a God too big to fail."*

This is where I want to encourage you: You can't keep hanging out with natural men, because they'll never understand where God is taking you. They don't understand why you pray the way you do, why you worship the way you do. They look at you in a funny way when you holler a little too loudly. They tilt their heads when your hands go up and tears fall down. But a spiritual man is dead to self, alive to Christ, and full of power.

**Say it: "I've got a weapon—I've got mass destruction living on the inside of me."**

Yes, mass destruction. Everything the Devil tries to throw at you, the Holy Ghost is about to shut down.

**Shout it: "I'm not natural!"**

I refuse to live another day thinking natural thoughts. I'm not made for the natural—I'm made for the supernatural.

Recently, I was praying, and the glory of God hit my office like a lightning bolt. I could have been raptured right then and there. I was in the presence of God. And the Lord spoke so clearly. He said, "People's logic has limited Me. I want to do so much more, but their small thinking and low revelation of the Greater One in them—it's limiting what I want to do. I want to do exceedingly, abundantly above all you could ask or think."

But your limited ability to think and your natural-mindedness have stopped God from doing the work that He wants to do for you. So today I declare: the natural part of me is dying. There's no more natural thinking—I am a supernatural being filled with the Spirit of God. And it grieves me when I look around at the world full of laughter and boldness, while the Church walks around defeated, depressed, dragging its feet like victims. You've got a bumper sticker on your car that says, "Jesus saves," but your face says, "I've lost everything."

When someone asks, "How are you?" and you reply, "Well, under the circumstances..."—that tells me you've lost your joy. But listen: The natural man is meant to submit to the man of the Spirit. The natural man has no joy, but the Spirit-man walks in power. When God breathed into man's nostrils, He didn't just give breath—He gave a part of Himself. That means wherever I walk, I carry the Ark of the Covenant. I shift atmospheres. Demons scatter when I step into the room.

The Bible says the natural man can't receive the things of the Spirit because they seem illogical. But there's a supernatural man—Jesus—who takes natural men and causes them to do impossible things. He told Peter, "Come, walk on the water." He didn't say, "Let's see if this works." No, He said, "Come" (Matthew 14:29), because the ability was already planted in Peter's spirit. Greater is He that is in you than anything that opposes you. The moment you get a revelation of who lives inside you, the Devil has a serious problem on his hands. I am the Devil's worst nightmare.

The world is laughing, drinking, dancing, and full of joy. But the Church? Too many are moping around, filled with anxiety and fear. But if you truly understood the indwelling power of the Holy Ghost, you'd know it's impossible to live "under the circumstances." In Him, you're always above and never beneath.

A great man of God once said, "Joy is serious business in Heaven." It's not just a smile. It's not shallow happiness. It's a Spirit-fueled weapon.

Let me tell you what joy is. Joy is supernatural. You were supposed to be weeping over your problems, but suddenly, God puts something *supernatural* on your *natural*. The Devil expected tears—but instead, you've got joy. Your natural mind doesn't understand it, but deep down, you know God is pulling you out. *"I'm coming through this."*

Joy is laughing in the face of adversity and declaring, *"I don't care what the Devil says—greater is He that is in me!"*

**Shout it: "JOY!"**

The joy I have is something the world didn't give to me, and the world can't take it away. But here's the problem: Too many people are looking to *others* for their joy. Looking to *stuff*. If your joy is in your car, your job, your house, or people—it'll vanish. But when your joy comes from God—the only constant—it *cannot* be stolen. This world is not my home. My joy is eternal.

I've got joy in me. It's a supernatural deposit—Heaven's business living on the inside. Romans 14:17 says the Kingdom of God is not in eating or drinking, but in *righteousness*, *peace*, and *joy in the Holy Ghost*. We all know righteousness. We've heard about peace. But few understand the joy of the Holy Ghost.

When that joy hits you, it flows like a fountain. Your mind might still say, *"I don't know what I'm going to do"*—but the indwelling Spirit bypasses logic and fills you with confidence. There is a well inside of you. It needs to be stirred—a well that won't run dry.

If you think you can live without the Holy Spirit, you are making the biggest mistake of your life. Hard times are coming to the world—but the Church is about to receive joy unspeakable and full of glory.

When you understand the indwelling power of the Holy Spirit, you stop seeing yourself as the victim. You become the *answer*—to your family, your church, and your generation. He takes the timidity out of you. He removes the fear, the depression, and the anxiety—and replaces them with His power.

That's why the Bible says *greater*. Greater means stronger. Greater means better. Greater means able. Greater is He that is in me than depression, anxiety, or fear. Greater is He that is in me than the Devil who roams this world. The Holy Spirit is stronger, wiser, and more powerful than the enemy—and He lives in me!

**Shout it again: "GREATER!"**

Jesus said, "It's better for you if I go, because when I do, I'll send the Helper" (John 16:7). That Helper is the Paraclete—the Advocate—who fights your case for you. When I don't know what to pray, the Spirit of God prays through me with groanings too deep for words.

Paul said, "When I pray in the Spirit, I stir up my most holy faith" (Jude 1:20).

### Say it: "I'm stirring up my most holy faith."

You've got to let the God inside you have faith through you. Because when the natural mind says, *"Give up,"* the Holy Spirit rises up and says, *"Let's go higher!"* That's why Paul said, *"I pray in the Spirit more than all of you"* (1 Corinthians 14:18)—because the greater One in him had faith for him.

When you hit your lowest valley, the Holy Ghost will carry you to the mountain top. I don't just have a gentle Spirit—I've got a fighter, an advocate, a sword, a fire, a mighty rushing wind living inside me. And He fights for me.

The Holy Spirit is my best friend. He's not distant, not passive, and not silent. He's present, powerful, and personal. He walks with me, talks with me, fights for me, and fills me with joy when the world says I should be broken. He lifts me up when I don't know how to pray. He gives me boldness when fear knocks on the door. He reminds me of who I am in Christ, and He never leaves.

You don't have to live a natural life when the supernatural is available. You don't have to walk in defeat when victory has already been given. Open your heart. Let the fire of the Holy Ghost consume every limit you've placed on God. Let Him be your comforter, your advocate, your power, your joy, and your closest friend. Today, everything can change—because He is here.

# Afterword

This is not the end—it's only the beginning.

If the Spirit of God has been stirring something in you as you read this book, that's no accident. That's the evidence of life—real life—rising up in your spirit. Something eternal. Something unstoppable.

This entire book has pointed you to one unshakable truth: you were never meant to live a powerless Christian life. You were never called to blend in with the world, to be silenced by fear, or to be crushed by circumstances. You were created to carry the fire of God, to walk in power, and to live from a place of intimacy with the Holy Spirit.

This is your moment.

You don't have to wait for a conference. You don't have to chase another man's anointing. You don't need to beg Heaven to move. Heaven *already moved*—when Jesus

## Afterword

ascended and sent the Holy Spirit to dwell in you. The same Spirit that raised Christ from the dead now lives in you. And that changes everything.

Let this be the season you stop playing small. Let this be the day you say, *"No more natural living—I am a supernatural vessel."* Refuse to settle for a life of spiritual dryness when the rivers of living water have been promised to flow from within you.

But everything you've just read hinges on one foundational truth: the Holy Spirit comes to dwell only in those who have received Jesus Christ as their Lord and Savior. This power, this victory, this joy—it all begins at the cross. If you can't point to a moment in your life when you confessed Jesus as Lord and believed in your heart that God raised Him from the dead, today is your day.

You don't need to wait. You can settle it right now by praying this simple prayer out loud:

> "Lord Jesus, I believe You died for me and rose again. I confess You as my Lord and Savior. I turn from my old ways and receive Your life. Fill me with Your Spirit. Make me a new creation. I give You everything. In Jesus' name, Amen."

If you prayed that prayer as a declaration of your faith in Jesus Christ, welcome to the family of God! You've just made the greatest decision of your life. Tell someone. Find a Bible-believing, spirit-filled church that teaches the whole gospel. And get ready—because your life will never be the same.

Don't stop here. Stir up the gift. Pray in the Spirit. Meditate on the Word. Worship like it's war. Live like Heaven is real—because it is. You were born for such a time as this.

And now that you know who you are... the Devil's got a real problem!

# Notes

## Chapter 6

i. The Greek word *dunamis* (δύναμις) refers to the *miraculous power* or *dynamic strength* of God. It is where we get the English word "dynamite," but its biblical meaning is even more explosive. *Dunamis* is the supernatural force that comes from the Holy Spirit—it empowers believers to live victoriously, perform miracles, cast out demons, heal the sick, and boldly witness for Christ. This power isn't just for apostles or special moments; it's for every believer who is filled with the Spirit (see Acts 1:8; Luke 24:49; 1 Corinthians 2:4).

*Dunamis* is the very energy of Heaven operating through a yielded vessel. It's not human effort—it's divine enablement.

## Chapter 9

i. The Greek word *rhema* (ῥῆμα) refers to a specific, spoken word from God that is revealed and made alive to a believer by the Holy Spirit. While *logos* generally describes the written Word of God (the Bible as a whole), *rhema* describes the *living voice* of God—His Word made personal, timely, and active in a specific moment. A *rhema* word is what leaps off the page during your reading, stirs your spirit in prayer, or is prophetically quickened in your heart. It is God speaking *now*, directly to you, and it carries the power to transform your thinking, build your faith, and guide your next step (see Romans 10:17; Matthew 4:4; John 6:63).

# About Wessel du Bruyn

Wessel du Bruyn is a passionate evangelist, revivalist, and founder of Wessel du Bruyn Ministries. Originally from South Africa, he now lives in Florida, United States, with his wife Eileen and their children, where they continue to minister globally. Known for powerful moves of the Holy Spirit—including signs, wonders, and healing—Wessel has carried the uncompromising gospel of Jesus Christ to over 80 nations.

From a young age, supernatural encounters and an unwavering pursuit of God's presence have marked Wessel's life. Bold demonstrations of the Spirit's power define his ministry and a burning desire to see believers awakened—not to religion, but to a daily, intimate relationship with the Holy Spirit.

Together, Wessel and Eileen carry a bold mandate: to win 700 million souls for Jesus. Their ministry features weekly television programs that reach audiences worldwide, equipping believers to walk in the fullness of the

Spirit and fulfill their divine calling. *Holy Spirit My Best Friend* is Wessel's debut book and a deeply personal invitation into the same life-altering friendship that fuels his life and mission.

Stay connected with Wessel du Bruyn Ministries through the official website. You'll find powerful teachings, service times, event information, and ways to partner with the ministry.

**www.wdbm.org**

Receive daily encouragement and stay up to date by following us on social media, and listen to life-transforming messages anytime, anywhere on Podbean:

**wdbministries.podbean.com**

instagram.com/wdbministries
facebook.com/wdbministries
youtube.com/@wesseldubruyn

www.ingramcontent.com/pod-product-compliance
Lightning Source LLC
Chambersburg PA
CBHW050033090426
42735CB00022B/3475